Soccer Dreams

Clare Hodgson Meeker

ILLUSTRATIONS BY Karen Luke Fildes

CO
CREATING ONE LLC
MERCER ISLAND, WASHINGTON

DEDICATION

•

To Tolossa Hassan, Andrea Gomez, and Vikram Vasan, whose soccer dreams inspired this story, and to our beloved Seattle Sounders. When you're learning to play soccer, you need someone to look up to.

I would like to thank the Communications staff at Seattle Seahawks/Seattle Sounders FC for their support of this project, including organizing the player interviews and photo gathering, particularly Mike Flood, Suzanne Lavender, Frank MacDonald, and Zac Kaplan. They are a great example of teamwork.

I would also like to thank Sigi Schmid, Fred Goodwin, Darren Sawatzky, David Griffiths, Tim Murray, Susie Rosenstein, and Erica Steinitz for their time and their wise coaching advice.

Special thanks to Anne Depue, Karen Schober, Karen Luke Fildes, Nancy Duncan, Roger Page, Wendy Crocker, Donna Bergman, Kathy Adler, and my husband, Dan Grausz, for helping me realize my dream for this book.

The quotes and profiles of the Seattle Sounders FC players are based on interviews with members of the 2009/2010 team, but their advice is timeless as we look forward to future seasons and new players.

Todo's story is fictional. The names, characters, places, and incidents are products of my imagination, and any resemblance to actual events or persons is coincidental.

Text copyright © 2011 by Clare Hodgson Meeker.
Illustrations copyright © 2011 Creating One LLC.
All rights reserved. Published by Creating One LLC. No portion of this book may be reproduced or transmitted in any form or by any means, electronic or mechanical, including photocopying, recording, or by any information storage and retrieval system without prior written permission from the publisher. For information contact Creating One LLC, 3215 74th Place SE, Mercer Island, Washington, 98040.

and team uniform for Seattle Sounders FC are registered trademarks and appear with permission from Seattle Sounders FC.

This book is a Major League Soccer Official Licensed Product. All Major League Soccer trademarks and copyright used by permission. All rights reserved.

First Edition
Printed in Canada
Distributed by Partners*west* Book Distributing, Inc.
1 2 3 4 5 6 7 8 9 10

Cover and interior design: Karen Schober Book Design, Seattle, Washington
Cover photo: Rod Mar (small), Clare H. Meeker (large)
Back cover photo: Getty Images
Interior illustrations: Karen Luke Fildes

Interior photos courtesy of Seattle Sounders FC, Getty Images, and the following photographers:
Title page: Julius Mwelu/Majority World
Marshall Hollis: Chapter 3, Coach Sigi Schmid, and Chapter 8, Four Spanish-Speaking Players
Chris Coulter: Chapter 12, U.S. Open Cup Champions 2010, and March to the Match.

Library of Congress Cataloging-in-Publication Data is available.
ISBN 978-0-615-43236-6

CO   CREATING ONE LLC
www.claremeeker.com
soccer@claremeeker.com

Contents

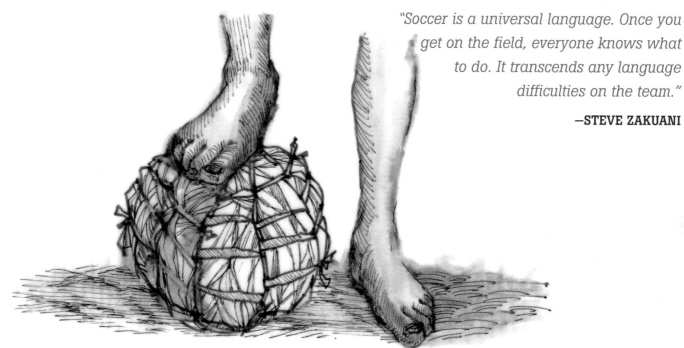

"Soccer is a universal language. Once you get on the field, everyone knows what to do. It transcends any language difficulties on the team."

—STEVE ZAKUANI

*Seattle Sounder Steve Zakuani
charged down the field,
outrunning the midfielders
with his long strides
and fast dribbling.*

*Weaving around the other team's defenders,
he had one opponent left to face—
the goalkeeper.
Zakuani faked to the right
and the goalkeeper pounced.*

*Then he quickly moved left
and blasted the ball
into the back of the net.
Goal!*

When I watch the Seattle Sounders play soccer,
I dream that I'm part of the team.
The players come from all over the world,
including Africa, where I was born.

My name is Todo.
I'm small for my age,
but I can run fast.
In my neighborhood in Nairobi, Kenya,
we played soccer every day after school
in an empty lot behind our apartment.
We used our shirts to mark the goal,
and a ball made of plastic bags
wrapped with nylon rope.

We wore sneakers, not cleats,
and sometimes no shoes at all
when we played on grass
against a team from
a different neighborhood.
You can run faster when you play in bare feet.

I organized the games,
so I was called the captain.
I could win the ball away
from anyone and take it
from one end of the field
to the other for a goal.

I even tried a bicycle kick once,
but fell flat on my back.
When we lost a game,
no one got upset.
Everyone knew we would be
back the next day to play again.

The day before my family left for America,
my friends gathered in a huddle
to say good-bye.
"Have you chosen a new captain?" I asked,
feeling a soccer ball–sized lump in my throat.

"First we have to make a new ball," they said,
handing me the one we had always played with as a gift.
"Even if they think you talk funny,
they will understand when you speak with your feet."

Defender Jhon Kennedy Hurtado Works to Play

Throughout his life, Jhon Kennedy Hurtado has worked hard to get what he wants. When Jhon was eight years old, he was invited to join an organized team in his hometown of Florida, Colombia. His family could not afford to buy him soccer shoes, so Jhon borrowed them from his friends to be able to play. Watching his older brother compete for Deportivo Cali, the famous Colombian football club, made Jhon take soccer more seriously. At age thirteen, he began to train with Deportivo Cali and took small jobs after school collecting cans for recycling to pay for cleats and bus tickets to practice. It was there that he met and became friends with another young player, Fredy Montero, who shared his dream of playing soccer professionally in the United States. After being named a 2009 MLS All-Star, Jhon had a season-ending knee injury in 2010 that he had to work back from. But his devotion to his teammates and fans and love for the game helped him to a full recovery.

Favorite warm-up: 5 on 2, or 4 on 2 in a circle, passing the ball.

Sounders FC tip: "In Spanish, we say, *Es la hora de poner el pecho a la brisa*, which means that it's time to put your chest to the wind—to face your problems and move on."

"The most important thing is, when you get opportunities, make the most of them."

—PATRICK IANNI

When we moved to Seattle,
I was not allowed to play outside
unless my older sister, Adila, came with me.
"I want to know you are safe," said my mother.
"We don't know anyone here."

Luckily, Adila loved playing soccer, too.
We would walk to Beacon Hill Playground,
kick off our shoes in the grass,
and play soccer in our bare feet.

Adila was a fierce defender.
She treated the ball as if it were her property
and I was a trespasser.
If I hesitated for one moment,
she would swoop in and sweep it away from me.
But the day Coach Dan stopped to watch us play,
I was ready for her.
I turned around the ball, keeping my back to her,
and rocketed it between the two trees
we used as goalposts.

"That's some fancy footwork
against a good defender," said the man
in the jogging suit, who looked
old enough to be my father.
"Do you two play on teams?"

"I go to middle school," said Adila,
looking surprised at his question.
"I only play soccer with my brother for fun."

"Well, you're good enough to play
on a middle school team.
And how old are you?" he said,
turning to me.

"I'm ten," I said, trying to look taller.

"I coach a team of boys your age.
We practice here in the park after school on Tuesdays.
How would you like to join us?" he asked.

"We will have to ask our parents first," answered Adila.

"Here is my name and phone number."
Coach Dan scribbled them down on a piece of paper.
"By the way, that's a great-looking ball," he said,
"but the one we use is harder.
You'll have to wear shoes."

"Yes, sir," I said,
tossing the plastic ball into the air to celebrate.
I would meet other kids who liked to play soccer
and Adila would not have to look after me.
What I really wanted to say to Coach Dan was
thank you for noticing me.

Forward Fredy Montero's Dancing Feet
●

On April 22, 2010, when Fredy Montero made his second goal of the second season on an incredible free kick from forty-one yards away, he kicked up his heels in a celebratory dance. "Soccer is for fun when you're young. It should start as recreation for kids and then gradually get more competitive."

Born in Colombia, Fredy dreamed of someday playing with Deportivo Cali, the famous Colombian football club that his hero, Carlos Valderrama (known in Spanish as El Pibe, or "The Kid"), played for. "I had a poster of El Pibe on my bedroom wall and watched his games on TV."

At age thirteen, Fredy left home to begin training to play professional soccer with the Deportivo Cali team. Following in his hero's footsteps, Fredy is the same height as El Pibe, five feet nine inches; quick and light on his feet like a Latin dancer; and always dangerous in the penalty box.

Favorite warm-up: Competition in shooting goals.

Proudest moments: Scoring two goals in the opening game of the first season and being named the MLS Newcomer of the Year in 2009.

Every Position Is Important

"I started out playing midfield. I tried goalie, too, but I ended up playing forward. I liked scoring goals more than stopping them."

—FREDY MONTERO

The following Tuesday
I came to practice,
expecting to play forward,
but Coach Dan had other plans for me.

"I'd like you to meet Todo,"
Coach Dan said to the team.
"He just moved here from Kenya."

"What position does he play?"
asked a tall blond boy,
bouncing a soccer ball on his knee.
"We've already got a goal scorer."
Nervous laughter floated up
from the rest of the team.

"Todo is fast and a good striker
like you, Peter," said Coach Dan.

"But we need defenders
who can clear the ball from our goal
and get it to the forwards' feet.
It's good to try playing different positions
to find out what you're best at."

"Isn't Todo a little small to be a defender?" smirked Peter.

I looked at Coach Dan.
He hadn't asked for Peter's opinion,
but was that what everyone was thinking?

"I'll try defense," I said,
trying to sound tougher than I felt.
"I just want to play."

"That's the spirit," said Coach Dan,
giving me the thumbs-up.
"There are extra uniforms, shin guards,
and a bucket of used cleats
in the back of my van.
Welcome to the team."

That night, I laid my new uniform
out on the bed
and put the plastic ball
away in the closet.
This was more than a pickup game.
I was part of a real team now—
whether Peter liked it or not.

Coach Sigi Schmid's Fingertip Feel for the Game

•

With two MLS Cup titles to his name, Sigi Schmid is one of the most successful coaches in the history of Major League Soccer. If you ask him his secret, he will tell you that it's about using "fingertip feelings," an expression from Germany, the country where he was born.

"Your instincts have to guide you. You can't go in with a pre-cut plan. You have to stay true to yourself and show the players you care. Be honest without being brutally honest. And if you pass on your passion and love for the game, that's more than any skill lessons you can give them."

Sigi grew up in Torrance, California, playing and watching soccer at the L.A. Coliseum, which hosted international games. At twelve, he met Pele, the world-famous Brazilian soccer player, when his team walked onto the Coliseum field after Sigi's team played in a pregame show.

"I had a soccer ball in my hands, and Pele asked me for it. He juggled the ball on his knee and then passed it to me. I juggled it and kicked it back to him. It's something I'll always remember."

Sounders FC tip: "Give every player a strength that sets them apart from the rest of the group. Everyone has something in the game they enjoy. Find that player's strength, and build around it."

Set Goals

"You need to know what you want to accomplish."

—KASEY KELLER

My father said we moved to Seattle
so that Adila and I could get a better education.
But it was hard to listen in class
when the students kept talking back to the teacher.

In Kenya, you could be punished for
arguing with an adult,
so I kept silent.
But then the teacher asked me
what continent Kenya is in.

"Kenya is in Africa," I answered.

"Kenyaaa is in Aaafrica," crooned Peter,
making fun of my accent.
The classroom erupted in giggles.

I cringed as the teacher silenced the class.
"That's not funny, Peter," she said.
"We should all try to make Todo feel welcome."
Her defending me only made things worse.

Recess could not come fast enough.
I grabbed a soccer ball from the gym
and dribbled out to the field
to practice shooting.
The moment my foot touched the ball,
I felt like I could breathe again.
Playing on a grass field instead of dirt
was the only good thing I could say about school.

"I bet you can't hit that pole ten times
in a row," said a girl I recognized from class.
She wore a bright green Sounders sweatshirt.

"Like this." She took the ball and kicked it hard
at a metal fence post a few yards away.
It ricocheted back and she kicked it again,
eight . . . nine . . . ten times in a row.

"Now it's your turn," she said,
handing it back to me.

I aimed for the pole,
but each time I kicked,
the ball came back at a different angle
and finally got away from me.
"How did you do that?" I asked,
stopping to catch my breath.

"Practice," she said.
"But you're not bad
for a guy who talks weird.
My name's Anna.
I hear you and Peter are on the same team.
He's a ball hog, you know."

"But is he good?" I asked.

"Yeah, he's good," said Anna,
"but he's not a team player.
We used to play soccer together
at recess in fourth grade.
Now I play up a year on a girls' team."

"I never saw a soccer team for girls in Kenya.
It would be fun to watch your team sometime," I said,
thinking Adila would want to see them, too.

"Most boys don't like to play girls' teams," said Anna.
"They think we're not enough of a challenge."

If the rest of your team is as good as you, I thought,
that's enough challenge for me.

I grabbed the ball as the recess bell rang.
"By the way," I said. "I'm a Sounders fan,
too. Seattle . . ."

". . . Sounders," Anna chanted back,
as we headed inside.

Zakuani Sets a Fast Pace

●

Before every game, Steve Zakuani looks at the scar on his leg and remembers the moped accident as a teenager in England that almost ended his dream of playing professional soccer.

"My father asked the doctor how long [it would be] before I could play soccer again, and the doctor said I would have to learn to walk again first."

Steve thought about giving up his dream, but his mother hid his crutches so he would have to walk to get them, and helped him get his strength back. "Once I got back to playing, the thrill came back. To this day, that's the only place I feel that feeling, when I'm on the field with the fans screaming."

Sounders FC tip: "Look up before you shoot, and aim where the goalie isn't looking."

Practice Hard

"Work harder than the next person
. . . it's contagious!"
—TYRONE MARSHALL

It was clear right from the warm-up
that our team had a problem.
"If you don't want to run,
you're in the wrong sport,"
Coach Dan shouted
at the players who were
joking around as we jogged
and dribbled balls
between the plastic cones.

Maybe I *was* weird
like Anna had said,
but I liked to run hard.

"This isn't fun," said a boy
who was bigger than the others
and had sat down to retie his shoes.
I noticed his hands and feet were huge.

Forward Mike Fucito's Steady Practice Pays Off

Mike Fucito's game-winning goal in the final minutes against the Kansas City Wizards in April 2010 sent shock waves through Qwest Field but was no surprise to his teammates, who practice with him every day.

"I just want to thank the coaches for putting me in and giving me a shot and believing in my game, [and] my teammates for their support."

In Concord, Massachusetts, where he grew up, Mike's skill and hard work on the soccer field inspired his teammates in both high school and college to elect him team captain. But his all-out playing style also brought injuries that forced him to spend time on the sidelines.

"It gives me a good perspective, and I learned some things from watching."

Whether Mike gets to start in a game or is substituted in at the end, his positive attitude always makes a difference.

"Wherever they see me best being able to help the team is where I feel the most comfortable. I just like being on the field."

"I know you can kick the ball really well, John,"
Coach Dan said to the boy.
"I'm going to put you and Todo
together on defense.
With your strength and his speed,
you two will make great partners."

Coach Dan had John and me
play a two-on-one drill
against Peter.

"Remember to play
with strength and *garra,*
like Sounder Ozzie Alonso says," said Coach Dan.

"What is *garra*?" John whispered to me.

"I think it means to fight fiercely
in Spanish," I whispered back.

"That I can do," said John.
"Let's go!"

Peter looked surprised
at the sudden change in John's pace.
He hesitated just long enough
for me to swoop in and
sweep the ball away from him.

"Nice job," said Coach Dan.

"Having fun yet?" I asked
my new partner.

"You bet!" smiled John
as we ran to the back of the line.

Peter glared at me,
but I wasn't worried.
The murmurs from the rest of the team
told me we had impressed them, too.

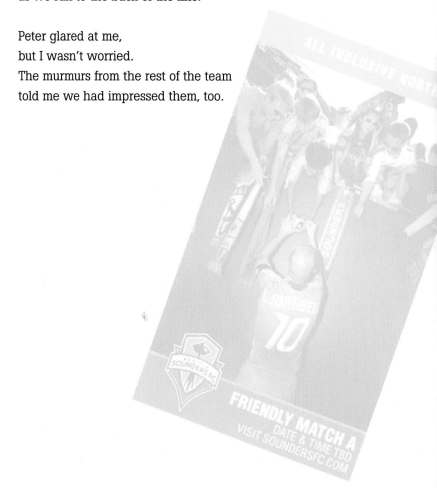

Talk to Each Other

Coach Dan was right.
John and I got along well on defense
as we started playing games
against other teams.
I liked seeing the whole field
and planning our attack,
when to fight for the ball
and when to fall back.

Coach Dan asked John to play goalkeeper.
Standing tall with his hands stretched wide,
he looked even bigger in the goal.

"I've got it!" John would shout
and throw himself at the ball.
I decided that when it comes to playing goalie,
size does make a difference.

When John made a save,
he liked to kick the ball as far as he could,
walloping it over the 50-yard line.
But that's when things got confusing.

It was painful to watch the midfielders
let the ball fly past them
and hear the other forwards yell,
"Give the ball to Peter,"
instead of going for it themselves.

The opposing players quickly figured out
that Peter was the guy to mark.
They ganged up on him
every time he got the ball,
giving him no chance to score.

Coach Dan sighed
after another nil-nil game.
"You've got to talk to each other
to create chances to score.
If you see an open space,
fill it, and call out for the ball.
We need other players
to pass to, besides Peter.
Don't wait for someone else to
do the job for you," he said.

If only Coach Dan would let me play forward,
I thought, *I know I could make a difference.*

Goalkeeper Kasey Keller Anchors the Defense

Born on an egg farm in Olympia, Washington, Kasey Keller decided at age thirteen that he wanted to focus on soccer and become a goalkeeper. "Being tall and having big hands definitely helps. I grew up in a sports family. My father played baseball for Washington State. He knew nothing about soccer. But baseball wasn't my strength."

Kasey went through the Washington Youth Soccer system from district to state to regionals to nationals. After college, he was invited to play professionally in England and around Europe, where he competed for sixteen years before returning home to captain the MLS Seattle Sounders.

What a goalkeeper thinks about: "You're continually changing your angle to be in the right position so that if the ball does break out, you are in the right spot. You're also trying to organize people to make sure they're aware of where other players are."

Sounders FC tip: "You're going to make mistakes, and those mistakes will cause goals. How do you bounce back from that? You have to have confidence in your own ability that you're going to save a lot more than you're going to give up."

"You have to be a little bit crazy to be a goalkeeper—willing to put your face places where you really don't want to."

—KASEY KELLER

I cornered Anna at school the next day.
"Do you know about playing defense?" I asked.

"I know I don't want to play goalie again," she said,
opening her mouth to show me a missing tooth.
"I was so worried about losing this tooth
that I let a goal in.
I like being a defender better anyway.
I get more time on the ball."

"But what about when the action
is at the other end of the field?" I asked.
"Don't you have to stay back near the goal?"

"Not always," said Anna.
"The Seattle Sounder defenders
can be just as dangerous
at the other end of the field,
helping to score a goal."

"Isn't it risky to leave
your own goal less protected?"

"Not if you're quick
and run back fast,
when the other team gets the ball."

"I'm not sure what Peter would do
if I moved into his forward territory," I said.

Anna rolled her eyes.
"You're not afraid of Peter, are you?" she asked.

"On my team,
I lead the charge up the field
to get the offense going.
Our coach always says,
'There's no "I" in soccer.'
You go where the team needs you."

Anna was right.
We needed to start acting like a team.
Maybe if I organized a scrimmage
against Anna's team,
it would make us work together to win.

Defender James Riley Gives Everything He's Got

James Riley helps his team every time he plays. In the two years he has been with the Seattle Sounders FC, he has played more minutes than any other player besides goal-keeper Kasey Keller, and has racked up an impressive record of assists and even goals.

"I work hard for my teammates . . . not really scoring goals but just solidifying and doing my bit day in and day out."

Growing up in Colorado in a single-parent family, James and his younger sister learned from their mother the importance of helping people without expecting anything in return. He also benefited from a caring soccer community, which he honors to this day with his solid effort on the pitch and his volunteer work in the community.

"I know if it wasn't for families in Colorado Springs picking me up from practices and taking me to games, there's no way I would be where I am today, so I definitely try to give back."

Sounders FC tip: "Always try to think steps ahead . . . and be a leader on the team."

Create Chances to Score

opposing defense
forward
midfielder
defender

forward
defender
defender
goalie

"It's not always about scoring yourself, but keeping the ball in play so if the other team's goalie does not make the save, your teammate can knock it in."

—PATRICK IANNI

Coach Dan liked my idea.
He announced it to the team
at the next practice.

"Girls play smart
and so can we.
Let's talk about strategy.
Heh, I'm a poet," said Coach Dan,
laughing at his own joke.
Everybody else groaned.

Coach Dan pulled out his clipboard
and drew three X's on a sheet of paper.
"When you watch the Sounders
move the ball up the field,
it's all about triangles," he said.
"The guy with the ball is
looking for someone to pass to.
The idea is to get yourself open
so you can receive the pass.
Then a new triangle forms around you."

"Isn't it faster to just kick the ball
up the field?" asked John.

"But then you have no control
over which team gets it first," said Coach Dan.
He put his clipboard down,
grabbed a ball, and tapped it over to me.

"Todo, pretend that you are Sounder
defender James Riley, and you've
just won the ball away from me.
Show me what you are going to do."

I started dribbling up the field,
looking for someone to pass to.
"Okay, midfielders," said Coach Dan,
"you are Sounders Osvaldo Alonso
and Alvaro Fernandez.
Find an open space and let Todo,
I mean James Riley, know
you're ready to receive his pass."

The midfielders scattered
away from Coach Dan
like pinballs shot from a spring.
I passed the ball to the midfielder
who was farthest up the field,
then ran to form a new triangle around him.

Midfielder Osvaldo Alonso Never Gives Up

●

Osvaldo Alonso's dogged determination to win the ball and pass it to the forwards' feet has earned him a reputation as a fierce competitor on the pitch. "I have always focused on giving it my best, playing with strength and *garra*, always maintaining that spirit of fierceness in order to win."

He has already dedicated many years to perfecting his game, having represented his state in Cuba at age eleven and been selected for the Cuban national team when he was seventeen. But it was his love of soccer and his dream of playing internationally that led him to leave Cuba and defect to the United States in 2007.

"Baseball is a bigger sport in Cuba. I hope to show people [how great soccer is] and keep on playing how I'm playing."

Favorite warm-up: 5 on 2.

Sounders FC tip: "You can't lose hope 'til the final whistle blows. Then learn from your mistakes. Focus on the next game, and work on the reasons why you lost."

I was in the forwards' territory
when I heard Peter call for the ball.
He was hovering in the penalty box
on the other side of Coach Dan.
I wanted to take a shot
and show the team what I could do,
but Peter was closer to the goal.

So when Coach Dan came at me
I crossed the ball to Peter instead,
and he launched it into the goal.

"What took you so long, Kenya?" shouted Peter,
with a sly smile.

He knew what I had been thinking.
As the players high-fived each other,
Coach Dan grinned.
"Now that's what I call teamwork!" he said.

"Think of the team first. Don't get angry."

—OSVALDO ALONSO

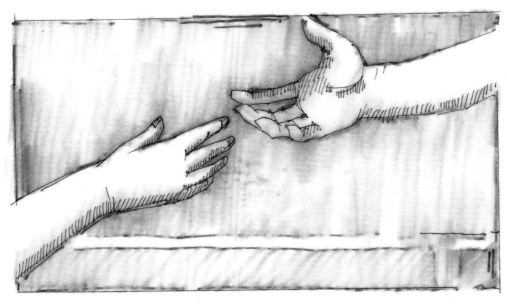

It was not easy convincing my parents
to watch our scrimmage against Anna's team.
They did not like the idea of girls
playing competitive sports.

But in the end, they came
with my sister to watch me play.
"I recognize a few of the girls
from my school," Adila said to me,
looking pleased.
"I didn't know they played soccer."

Coach Dan called us into a huddle
before the game started.
"Each of you brings something
special to this team," he said.
"We've got good passers, strong kickers,
fast runners, and smart finishers.
If you work together,
we can win this game.
Don't be afraid to go
one-on-one for the ball.
But if you lose, don't get upset.

Just move on to the next play.
Now go out there and have fun,
and may the triangle force be with you."

The girls took control of the ball right away.
The forwards were tall and looked older
as they charged down the center of the field,
passing the ball whenever we moved to block them.

John shifted back and forth in the
goal, preparing for them to strike.
Suddenly, he yelled, "Watch out on your right!"
as the ball was passed to Anna on the outside line,
and she sprinted by me.

I ran to intercept the ball
and got tangled in Anna's feet.
The ball sprang loose as we
both fell down, and another girl kicked it into the goal.
The girls' team went wild.

Anna stood and offered me a hand up,
but I refused to take it.
"Suit yourself," she said
and walked away.

I got up and walked back to John.
He looked pretty upset.
"I can't believe I let them

get a goal," he said,
kicking a clump of grass.

I was not feeling proud of myself either
at that moment.

Midfielder Roger Levesque Is "Ever Ready"

Roger Levesque earned the nickname "Ever Ready Roger" for being able to come into the game in the last minutes and make a difference.

"They say luck is where opportunity meets preparation. It starts on the practice field, just coming out working hard and competing. Sigi's going to make decisions about who plays and who doesn't. It's the coach's right. He does what he thinks is going to make the team win. Just being ready for that opportunity is my job at this point."

Roger quickly became a star athlete in his hometown in Maine, winning state Player of the Year in both soccer and basketball in high school. Soccer and the West Coast eventually won out. After playing four years at Stanford University and leading his college to a championship in his senior year, Roger joined the Sounders team in the United Soccer League and made the jump to the MLS Seattle Sounders FC.

Sounders FC tip: "You have to prove yourself every time you step on the field."

Anna's surprise move had shaken me up,
but I should not have let it get to me.

"It wasn't your fault," I said to John.

"It's the *team's* job to
prevent goals, and
we let you down.
The girls' team is good.
We just have to be better."

Give All You've Got

"Don't think about winning. Do what you have to do to the best of your ability. Focus on the process, and let the outcome take care of itself."

—STEVE ZAKUANI

"It's time to get creative," said Coach Dan after listening to Peter and the team vent at half-time.
"Todo, I'm moving you to the center of the field to get our passing action going. John, you're doing great as goalie. Let's add more defenders to help you."

John's face lit up at the unexpected compliment.
"We won't let you down," he said.

"What about me, Coach? Where should I be?" asked Peter.
Was this just another way to get attention, I wondered, *or did Peter really think the team had forgotten him?*

Coach Dan put his arm around Peter.
"I'm counting on you and Todo
to work together," he said.
"We've got a lot better chance of winning
when you act like you two are on the same side."

The girls came out in the second half
with even more energy.
I tried every trick I could think of
with the ball—
turning around it,
changing direction,
and finally passing it back to the defense
to get our triangle action going.

Suddenly I heard Peter yell, "I'm open!"
He had gone behind our defenders
to receive the pass and run.
Peter sprinted up the field with the ball
like Sounder Steve Zakuani,
weaving a path through the midfield and beyond.

I could see that Anna's eyes were fixed on Peter.
She was waiting to make her move
until he was closer to the goal.
If I moved to the outside
and was ready when she attacked him,
would Peter pass the ball to me?

I ran to the right and turned around
just in time to see the ball come at me.
I kicked up my leg, aiming left
toward the goal,
and fell flat on my back.

The next moment, I heard cheering
and Anna was standing over me.
"I can't believe you scored
with a bicycle kick,
just like Patrick Ianni," she said.

She reached out her hand again,
and this time I took it gratefully.
I was stlll feeling kind of dizzy
when the team came running up to me.
"You did it," said Peter.

"You mean we did it," I said,
beaming at the team.

Peter looked at Anna.
"You guys are good," he said,
"but of course you know that."

"It's nice to hear you say it," said Anna.
It was the first time I'd seen her blush.

After the game, I brought Anna over
to meet Adila.
"I hear you're good at soccer," said Anna.
"You should play with our team."

Adila and I looked nervously at our parents,
not knowing what they would say next.
"I got an education today," said my father,
"watching you girls whip my son's team into shape.
I leave it to Adila to decide, but I think she could not find
a better group of friends to play with."

Forward Blaise Nkufo's Magical Hat Trick

On September 18, 2010, barely two months after he joined the team, Blaise Nkufo set a Sounders FC record for scoring not once, not twice, but three times in the same game against the Columbus Crew. That's called a hat trick. The Sounders FC won by a score of 4-0.

Joining a team in the middle of the season can be challenging, even for a player with his experience. Blaise had just played in the 2010 World Cup for the Swiss national team, because he was raised in Switzerland after his family left the Democratic Republic of the Congo when he was seven. He was also named the Dutch Club's top marksman of all time after seven years with the FC Twente team. Playing soccer in America meant having to get used to a different style of play.

"MLS is a physical league. But every competition has its specific skills. My concern is to adapt quickly with my new team players, and that will be key to me."

Sounders FC tip: "As a striker, you have to believe you can score goals. But I'm here to help the team."

11

"Guys will fight for each other on the field when they like each other off the field."

—JAMES RILEY

The 1–1 game against the girls
was a turning point for our team.
Once we got our triangles working,
our team was unstoppable.

Peter no longer acted like
he owned the offense.
He started assisting other players
who stepped up to carry the ball.

Coach Dan continued to play me
both on defense and in the midfield.
I couldn't decide which position I liked better,
helping to make goals or prevent them.

"Don't worry," said Coach Dan,
"you've got plenty of time to figure out
which position you're best at.
We're lucky you're good at both
because you inspire the team."

With more wins than losses,
we made it to the championship,
but John got sick and could not come
to the final game.
I played defense,
but without our fearless goalkeeper,
we could not prevent a last-minute strike
from reaching its mark.

After the game, our team stayed on the field.
It hurt to lose, but hurt more to know that
this was our last game.
The season was over.

Anna and Adila had watched
the game together and
came over to cheer us up.
"Win or lose, you guys still
had a great season," Anna whispered.
"I'm hoarse from cheering."

"Our girls' team promises to give you
an even tougher time next year," said Adila,
"with Anna and me on defense."

Coach Dan smiled.
"Congratulations, Adila,
on making the team," he said.
"Anna is right. It's not just about winning.

I'm proud of each one of you
for giving your all for the team.
And I have a little surprise for you."
He pulled a batch of tickets out of his pocket.
"We're all going to a Sounders game."

Sitting in my room that night,
I was still thinking about the game we lost
when I saw my plastic ball lying in the closet.

Defender Patrick Ianni's Bicycle Kick

●

On July 11, 2009, Patrick Ianni scored the game-winning goal against his former team, the MLS Houston Dynamo, using a bicycle kick. "I remember trying the bicycle kick for fun when I was eight years old at a soccer camp. The more you practice it, the easier it gets."

Patrick's older brother, who played soccer for UCLA, got him started with the game. "I played other sports, but watching my brother succeed steered me in the direction of soccer."

Favorite warm-ups: Jumping up for headers and directing the ball to the players' hands. Playing soccer tennis before a game: "We string tape between two chairs. Roger hits the ball up to me, and sometimes I do bicycle kicks to get it over."

Sounders FC tip: "You have to have a competitive drive and a balance of intelligence and intensity to succeed."

I picked it up and tossed it in the air.
My friends in Kenya were right, I thought.

*This ball helped me make new friends.
Who needs a trophy? There's always next year.*

12

"Keep the spirit of happiness for the game."

—JHON KENNEDY HURTADO

Our team piled out of Coach Dan's van
at the entrance to Qwest Field.
A sea of people moved around us,
some with painted faces
and hair dyed blue and green,
waving Sounders scarves
and dancing to the beat of the marching drums.

A man wearing a headset took us
through the doors to an open space

behind the stadium seats.
Anna's team was already there.
The man gave us Sounders T-shirts
and spoke to the whole group.

"Welcome, members of our Dream Team.
The Seattle Sounders FC selected you
to walk out on the field with them today
because your coach told us you know
what it means to work together as a team.

In a few minutes I'll take you down to the tunnel,
where you will be paired up with a player.
So if you have any burning questions for them,
now is the time to ask."

"I hope I get to walk out
with Kasey Keller," said John.
"I'd ask him if he ever had
to miss an important game."

"I'd like to stand next to
Fredy Montero," crowed Peter.
"I bet we'd get the loudest cheer."

"You're always looking for attention," teased Anna.
"I'd be happy walking out with any one of them.
They're all sooooo awesome!"

It felt good to laugh
because I was nervous.
Would I even be able to talk
when we met the players
face to face?

But when we reached the tunnel
and I saw the team waiting for us,
I walked up to Steve Zakuani
and shook his hand.

"I'm Todo," I said.
"I just moved here from Kenya."

Steve smiled. "I was born in the Congo,"
he said, in an accent just like mine.
"Is there anything you want to ask me
before we walk out on the field?
Thirty thousand screaming fans make a lot of noise."

Suddenly I blurted out
something I had never told anyone before.
"I dream of being a professional soccer player like you.
When you were my age, did you have soccer dreams, too?"

"Yes, I had soccer dreams, and I still do," said Steve.
"Right now, my dream is that our Sounders team
will win the playoffs."
Then he leaned down and whispered,
"I also dream that someday an African team will
win the World Cup, and I'll be playing for them."

As we walked out onto the field,
the roar of the crowd was amazing.
In that moment, I felt like I was part of the team,
and I believed my dream would someday come true.

Forward Nate Jaqua Trains to Stay in Top Form

●

Nate Jaqua knows how it feels to have to sit on the sidelines because of an injury.

"It's tough not being able to go mix it up with the guys and play. That's why we do it. That's what makes it fun."

Nate's father played football professionally. "My dad got really beat up playing, so my mom steered us away from football right at the beginning."

Nate chose soccer as his sport early on. But like his father, he dreamed about being the best at his sport. "I always wanted to be a number 10, a playmaker, a Ronaldo [the Brazilian player known for his goal scoring]."

At six feet four inches, Nate is one of the tallest players in the league and one of the team's leading scorers.

Favorite music to prepare for a game: Reggae. "[Bob Marley] gets me in a nice mellow zone. Before a game, I kind of need to relax."

Soccer is for fun when you are young.

Do you recognize which future Sounders FC players these are?

From the left: Fredy Montero, Mike Fucito, Roger Levesque, Patrick Ianni